Collins

Easy Lea

English

Ages 7–9

an apple

a banana

Shareen Mayers

How to use this book

This book is for parents who want to work with their child at home to support and practise what is happening at school.

Tips

- Your child should work in a quiet, comfortable place, away from distractions.
- Help with reading the instructions where necessary and ensure your child understands what to do.
- Tackle one topic at a time and give your child opportunities to practise.
- Help your child compose sentences orally before writing them.
- Encourage your child to check his/her answers.
- Discuss with your child what he/she has learnt.
- Discuss favourite activities.
- Reward your child with lots of praise and encouragement.

Parents' notes

At the bottom of each page you will find a footnote. **Supporting your child** explains how you can help your child practise the activity. **Taking it further** suggests additional activities and encourages discussion about what your child has learnt.

> The vocabulary that your child should know and use by the end of this book includes:
>
> conjunction   direct speech   inverted commas (or speech marks)
>
> prefix   preposition   subordinate clause

We hope that you and your child enjoy working through this book.

ACKNOWLEDGEMENTS

The author and publisher are grateful to the copyright holders for permission to use quoted materials and images.

p.5, p.13 © 2008 Jupiterimages Corporation; p.14 © Shutterstock.com/LukoS; p.28 *The Woman who Fooled the Fairies* cover, HarperCollins*Publishers* © 2005 Rose Impey and Nick Schon; p.28 *How to be a Pirate* cover, HarperCollins*Publishers* © 2004 Scoular Anderson

Every effort has been made to trace copyright holders and obtain their permission for the use of copyright material. The author and publisher will gladly receive information enabling them to rectify any error or omission in subsequent editions. All facts are correct at time of going to press.

Published by Collins
An imprint of HarperCollins*Publishers*
77–85 Fulham Palace Road
London W6 8JB

© HarperCollins*Publishers* Limited

ISBN 9780007559862

First published 2014

10 9 8 7 6 5 4 3 2 1

British Library Cataloguing in Publication Data.

A CIP record of this book is available from the British Library.

Publishing Manager: Rebecca Skinner
Author: Shareen Mayers
Commissioning and series editor: Charlotte Christensen
Project editor and manager: Tracey Cowell
Cover design: Susi Martin and Paul Oates

Inside concept design: Lodestone Publishing Limited and Paul Oates
Text design and layout: Q2A Media Services Pvt. Ltd
Artwork: Rachel Annie Bridgen, Q2A Media Services
Production: Robert Smith
Printed and bound by Printing Express Limited, Hong Kong

5 EASY WAYS TO ORDER

1. Available from www.collins.co.uk
2. Fax your order to 0844 576 8131
3. Phone us on 0844 576 8126
4. Email us at education@harpercollins.co.uk
5. Post your order to: Collins Education, Freepost GW2446, Glasgow G64 1BR

Contents

Prefixes

Prefixes are groups of letters that are added to the beginning of words to change their meaning.

Un- and dis-

Adding un– or dis– to a word gives it a negative meaning.

- Write un– in front of these words to change their meaning.

    _un_ well

    _un_ lucky

    _un_ tidy

    _un_ grateful

- Write dis– in front of these words to change their meaning.

    dis obey

    dis agree

    dis appoint

    dis appear

Choosing un- and dis- words

- Choose from the un– and dis– words above to complete these sentences.

    I felt really _un well_ so I went to visit my doctor.

    I am sorry to _dis appoint_ you but we have no pencils left in the shop!

    My sister's room looked very _un tidy_, so I tidied it for her.

Supporting your child Help your child to write words with common prefixes.

4

Re– means 'again' or 'back'

- Write re– in front of these words to change their meaning. Then cover each word and write it in full.

_____do _____

_____fresh _____

_____turn _____

_____appear _____

_____decorate _____

Jolly joke

Why was the biscuit unhappy?

Because his mum had been a wafer so long!

Super– means 'big'

- Write super– in front of these words to change their meaning. Then cover each word and write it in full.

_____market _____

_____man _____

_____natural _____

_____star _____

**super = big
above
more than**

- Now write the super– words above next to their meaning.

a famous and well-known singer _____

something that is beyond nature _____

a shop that is bigger than most _____

a man with more-than-ordinary powers _____

Taking it further Look up the four prefixes on these pages in a dictionary. Then list ten words that start with **un–**, **dis–**, **re–** and **super–**.

–tion and –sion suffixes

Suffixes are groups of letters that are added to the ends of words.

–tion is used if the root word ends in **t** or **te**, and is the most common ending.

–sion is used if the root word ends in **d/de** or **s/se**.

Examples:

Root word	–tion or –sion?
invent	invention
expand	expansion (the **d** has been removed)

There are some exceptions to these rules. For example, attend ⟶ attention and intend ⟶ intention. You just have to learn them!

–tion or –sion?

- Change these words by adding the correct –tion or –sion suffix. Remember to look carefully at how each root word ends before you add the suffix.
- Then rewrite the word in full in the space provided.

  Use the rules above to help you.

  inject _____

  _____

  extend _____

  _____

  act _____

  _____

  comprehend _____

  _____

  tense _____

Fill the gaps

● Complete the table. The first one has been done for you.

Root word	–sion or –tion?
<u>corrode</u>	corrosion
explode	_____
_____	hesitation
_____	infusion
complete	_____

● Now choose a word from the table to complete these sentences.

Without any _____ , David dived into the swimming pool.

I had to _____ my homework on time.

Write your own

● Write four sentences of your own.
● Use a –tion or –sion word in each sentence.

_____

_____

_____

_____

_____

_____

Taking it further   Encourage your child to look up the meanings of the **–tion** and **–sion** words on these pages. He/she can then use more **–tion** and **–sion** suffixes in his/her own writing.

–ture ending

If a word sounds as if it ends with **–chur**, it is often spelt **–ture**.

literature

puncture

capture

Before you write **–ture**, always check that it is not a root word ending with the **–er** suffix, for example, teacher (teach) and richer (rich).

Write the endings

• Finish these common words using the **–ture** ending.

pic_____   na_____

fu_____   mix_____

furni_____   adven_____

Supporting your child Check that your child understands when to spell words with **–ture** endings.

8

It helps to split long words into **syllables**, or separate 'beats'.

Every syllable must have a vowel (a, e, i, o, u). However, 'y' can act as a vowel sound too, for example, g**y**m, fl**y** and bab**y**.

Syllables

- Split these –ture words into separate syllables. The first one has been done for you.

capture   *cap-ture* _____

creature   _____

culture   _____

fixture   _____

fracture   _____

moisture   _____

Write your own

- Write four sentences of your own.
- Use a –ture word in each sentence.

_____

_____

_____

_____

_____

_____

_____

Taking it further   Encourage your child to use a dictionary to check the meanings of the **–ture** words on these pages that he/she is unsure of.

Apostrophes

This is an apostrophe: '.

Apostrophes can be used to show when a letter or letters have been taken out of a word. This is called a **contraction**. So if you want to write I am as I'm, you put in the apostrophe to show where the a is missing and then join the words together.

Apostrophes for possession are used to show that something belongs to someone or something. For example, **the coat belonging to the girl** is written as **the girl's coat**.

Apostrophes for contraction

● Draw lines to match the long form of each word to its short form.

Long form	Short form (contraction)
I am	she's
might have	I'll
I shall/will	couldn't
they are	would've
it is	doesn't
you are	it's
does not	you're
would have	won't
will not	we're
did not	I'm
could not	who's
we are	might've
she is	didn't
who is	they're

The cat is chasing its tail.

The cat's chasing its tail.

Supporting your child   Check that your child knows how to use apostrophes in his/her writing. It's easy to put the apostrophe in the wrong place, particularly in informal writing.

Never write of!

Remember: could've and would've are short forms of could have **and** would have**, not 'of'!**

● Look back at the words in long form on page 10. Write down the missing letters in these contractions.

could've _____

should've _____

might've _____

would've _____

Jolly joke

Doctor, Doctor. My wife thinks she's a clock!

Well, stop winding her up then!

Apostrophes for possession

● Rewrite each phrase, adding an apostrophe for possession to show who or what the object belongs to. The first one has been done for you.

the tail belonging to the dog — *the dog's tail*

the dinner belonging to the man — _____

the wheel belonging to the tractor — _____

the doll belonging to the child — _____

the pen belonging to the teacher — _____

the hump belonging to the camel — _____

Taking it further Suggest your child writes a conversation containing lots of contractions and then writes the full version of the words. Which version reads more naturally?

Articles (a, an, the)

a, **an** and **the** are called **articles**. They are used before a noun (people, place or thing) or an adjective (describing word).

a cat   **an** apple   **the** children

Where are the articles?

- Circle the articles (**a**, **an** or **the**) in these sentences.

  An apple a day is good for you.

  The school play started on time.

  The supermarket will open at 8am.

  An egg can be boiled before eating it.

Fill the gaps

- Write the correct articles (**a** or **an**) in front of these nouns.

  _____ pen   _____ pan   _____ pot

  _____ elephant   _____ bird   _____ arrow

- Write the correct articles (**a** or **an**) in front of these adjectives.

  _____ beautiful girl   _____ open book   _____ fiery dragon

  _____ amazing school   _____ delicious cake   _____ exciting play

- Complete this sentence using the correct articles (**a** or **an**).
  The girl found _____ gold ring in _____ old treasure box.

Supporting your child   The articles **a**, **an** and **the** are types of determiners. Help your child to remember that the article **a** comes before a word beginning with a consonant and **an** comes before a word beginning with a vowel. There are some exceptions to this rule, such as 'an hour', which has a silent **h**, and words beginning with **eu** or **u** when they make the 'ue' (as in 'you') sound, e.g. 'a European'. **The** is used to talk about a particular person or thing.

Prepositions

Prepositions are words that show the relationship between one thing and another. They are also used to describe relationships of time.

Exact times: **at**   He arrived **at** 3pm yesterday.

Days and dates: **on**   My birthday is **on** 10 November.

Future times: **in**   I will finish my shopping **in** two hours.

Where are the prepositions?

- Underline the prepositions (**at**, **on** or **in**) that show time in these sentences.

  The baby girl was born at 12 noon on Monday.

  They had a big party in August.

  She'll serve you in ten minutes.

  Her wedding was at 10am but she was an hour late.

Changing times

Prepositions can also show a change in time.

- Select the correct preposition from the box to complete these sentences.

before	after	during	because of	since

We ate our breakfast _____ going to the zoo.

I clean my teeth _____ I have eaten my supper.

I have been waiting here _____ 9am!

Jolly joke

Want to hear the story about the broken pencil?

I'm sure it has no point!

Taking it further Encourage your child to look at how prepositions and articles are used on signs, notices and advertisements, and in books. Be careful! Some signs are incorrect so your child should look out for mistakes.

Conjunctions

Sentences and parts of sentences can be joined by **conjunctions** such as **and**, **but** and **so**. For example, **and** can be used to link two words (apples **and** oranges) or to link sentences together.

Where are the conjunctions?

- Underline **and**, **but** or **so** in the following passage.

The ginger cat hurriedly chased after the tiny mouse but he was too fast! He speedily ran across the room so the cat could not find him. Later on, the mouse laughed at the cat and hid under the huge staircase.

Join the parts together

- Choose **and**, **but** or **so** to join the sentence parts together and make complete sentences.

Our school netball team tries really hard _____ we hardly ever win.

I would like to come _____ my mum won't let me!

We wanted to win the football match _____ we had to work as a team.

I will take off my boots _____ I don't make a mess!

I want to have pizza for dinner _____ ice cream for dessert.

Subordinate clauses

Other examples of conjunctions are **while**, **after**, **although**, **when** and **before**.

When **extra information** is added to a sentence after or before a conjunction, it is called a **subordinate clause**.

Where are the subordinate clauses?

- Circle the subordinate clauses in these sentences. The first one has been done for you.

  The girl was feeling unwell **after** she had eaten lunch.

  Although it was night-time, the street was full of people.

  The dog barked **when** he saw his owner.

  Before dawn, the silver spaceship landed somewhere in the woods.

  While they were sleeping, a rainbow arched across the sky.

Jolly joke

What are subordinate clauses?

Santa's helpers!

Join the sentences together

- Join the pairs of sentences with one of the conjunctions below to make one sentence with a subordinate clause. The first one has been done for you.

because	although

Jack went up the hill. He was very tired.

Jack went up the hill **although** he was very tired.

The footballer scored. The other team were playing well.

_____

The monkey looked bored. He wanted to live in the wild.

_____

I had to share my cake. My brother didn't have one.

_____

Taking it further   In your child's writing, check whether two separate sentences can be joined using a conjunction.

Direct speech

Inverted commas (or speech marks) are used to show words that are spoken. This is called direct speech.

The brown cow said, "How now!"

The black cow replied, "How now to you too!"

Highlight what people say

- In this passage, highlight all the parts that people say in one colour.

The teacher asked, "Which is farther away – China or the sun?"

"China," answered Milly.

"Why do you think that?" asked the teacher in surprise.

"Well, you can see the sun, but you can't see China," Milly replied.

- What punctuation is used within the inverted commas (speech marks)?

_____

- When do you start a new line?

_____

There are several rules for using inverted commas.

1 Start each new speaker on a new line, if it is a new sentence.

2 Put inverted commas around the words actually spoken.

3 Place punctuation connected with the direct speech **inside** the inverted commas.

4 If direct speech is followed by more text, end with a comma (not a full stop) inside the inverted commas.

Jolly joke

Why couldn't the pirate play cards?

He was sitting on the deck!

From speech bubbles to inverted commas

- Add inverted commas (or speech marks) to the speech bubbles. Then rewrite the speech bubbles as text with inverted commas in the space provided.

  Look back to the teacher's conversation with Milly on page 16 to help you.

_____

_____

_____

_____

_____

_____

_____

_____

_____

_____

_____

_____

Taking it further   Look carefully at how direct speech is written in books. Then, your child could rewrite parts of picture stories that he/she reads, using inverted commas (speech marks).

Verbs (to have)

Verbs can use the words **have** or **has** (e.g. **I have** and **she has**). These words talk about events that started in the past but they do not mention an exact time.

She went out to play. ——> She <u>has gone</u> out to play.

This is a different way of writing the simple past tense.

Where are the verbs (have or has)?

- In the sentences below, underline the verbs that do not show an exact time. The first one has been done for you.

They <u>have watched</u> television three times this week.

She has gone to the shops.

Her uncle has had an accident.

I have been to school today.

Fill the gaps 1

- Choose either **has** or **have** to complete these sentences.

I _____ been doing my homework.

Our daughter _____ learnt how to ride a bike.

_____ you made your bed already?

The singer _____ still not arrived.

Supporting your child Say sentences in the past tense and then say them again using the present perfect verbs **has gone** or **have been**. (For example, "I went to the park" becomes "I have been to the park".) This can be tricky for children to learn, so practising sentences orally will support their understanding.

Fill the gaps 2

- Choose either **has** or **have** to complete these sentences.

He _____ gone to the cinema.

The children _____ made a delicious cake.

The woman _____ not finished painting the wall yet.

I _____ bought some tickets to visit the adventure park.

Jolly joke

What's an eight-letter word that has one letter in it?

An envelope!

Changing sentences

- In these sentences, change **went** to **has gone** or **have been**. Notice how this changes the meaning of each sentence. The first one has been done for you.

He went out to play. ⟶ _He has gone out to play._

I went to the shops. ⟶ _____

She went to the museum. ⟶ _____

I went to the supermarket. ⟶ _____

Now write one sentence of your own using **have been** and one sentence using **has gone**.

_____

_____

_____

_____

_____

Taking it further   Encourage your child to start using the present perfect tense in his/her own writing.

Adverbs

Adverbs give extra information about verbs, saying how, when or where something happened.

This dog is growling **playfully**.

This dog is growling **fiercely**.

The adverbs, playfully and fiercely, tell us more about how the dog is growling.

Adverbs very often end in –ly.

Fill the gaps

- Choose suitable adverbs to complete these sentences.

The cat walked _____ across the steep roof.

People talk _____ in a library.

Matthew stroked his pet rabbit _____.

The cars raced _____ around the track.

The old man spoke _____ to the dog that had just trampled on his flowers.

Supporting your child   Check that your child understands that adverbs can make a piece of writing much more exciting. Remind him or her that adverbs do not always end in **–ly**. For example, words like **then**, **next** and **soon** tell us **when** something has happened.

- With a partner, take it in turns to think of an adverb, e.g. noisily, and then do different things in the style of that adverb. The other person has to guess which adverb you have thought of.

- Another way of playing this game is for the other person to set you tasks, which you then act out in the style of the adverb you thought of. They then try to guess your adverb.

Jolly joke

When is the vet busiest?

When it rains cats and dogs!

Adjectives and adverbs

- Make these sentences more interesting by adding **adjectives** (to describe the nouns) and **adverbs** (to extend the verbs). Rewrite the sentences in full. The first one has been done for you.

The monster roared.

The fierce monster roared wildly.

The boy made his bed.

_____

The dog was growling.

_____

The girl was singing.

_____

Taking it further   Look at some advertisements. Try to spot the adjectives and adverbs that make the descriptions sound more enticing.

Better adjectives

Nice is a boring word! There are much better adjectives you could use to describe what someone or something is like.

● Write out this story, replacing the word nice. These adjectives will help you.

| delicious fine lovely pleasant attractive |

It was a nice day. The elf had a nice breakfast and went for a nice walk in the garden. It was nice weather and the flowers looked very nice.

_____

_____

_____

Use your thesaurus

Do you have a thesaurus at school or at home, or are you able to access one online? It will give you lists of adjectives that have similar meanings. A dictionary will also help.

● List adjectives that you could use instead of these words.

beautiful _____

huge _____

small _____

spooky _____

Supporting your child   Adventurous adjectives are an easy way to make writing more interesting. Encourage your child to use a dictionary or thesaurus to help expand his/her vocabulary.

Describing characters

Interesting adjectives can make characters in a story come alive!

- Think of a story about four very different characters who live in a castle. Write descriptions of the four characters using full sentences. You can use your lists of adjectives from page 22 to help you.

The princess

The giant

The elf

The ghost

Action!

- Write a few lines about a typical day for the four characters. Use lots of interesting, descriptive adjectives.

_____

_____

_____

_____

Jolly joke

What is a spook's favourite ride?

A roller-ghoster!

Taking it further   Ask your child to write a longer story about the four characters, with plenty of rich vocabulary.

Characters, setting and plot

Characters

When you write a story, the first thing you need is characters.

- Invent some characters for a story you are going to write. Write the name of each character on the answer lines. Draw a picture of each character in the boxes.

Character 1 _____

Character 2 _____

Character 3 _____

Setting

**The setting means where and when your story happens.
Answer these setting questions about your story.**

- Where will you choose? _____

- Is it real or make-believe? _____

- When does it happen? _____

Supporting your child Before your child starts to write a story, always encourage him or her to make notes on the characters, setting and plot.

What's the plot?

The plot means what happens in the story. It often has a problem that is solved.

- Describe the plot of your favourite story.

_____

_____

_____

_____

Jolly joke

What do you call a song sung in an automobile?

A cartoon!

Plan the plot

- Now make notes for the plot of your own story. Remember to think about where and when something happens, and who is in your story. Put them under these headings.

Beginning	Problem	How it is solved (resolution)	Ending

Taking it further   When you read stories together, discuss the characters, the setting and the plot. Try to work out how the author planned his/her writing.

The structure of a story

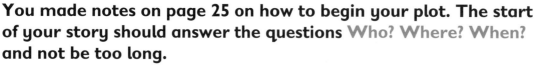

The beginning

You made notes on page 25 on how to begin your plot. The start of your story should answer the questions Who? Where? When? and not be too long.

● Write the beginning of your story.

_____

_____

_____

_____

The problem

The 'problem' section will be the longest part of your story, probably half of the whole length. It describes what happens in your plot.

● Write this section of your story. Continue on another sheet, if needed.

_____

_____

_____

_____

Supporting your child Encourage your child to use and refer to his/her plan on page 25 when writing the story.

The resolution

In the 'resolution' part of the story, the problem is solved.

- Write the resolution section of your story. Continue on another sheet, if needed.

_____

_____

_____

_____

_____

The ending

You must give your story a definite ending. Don't let the story just tail off.

Think about how your reader will feel at the end.

- Write the end of your story.

_____

_____

_____

_____

_____

Jolly joke

Why did the burglar take a shower?

He wanted to make a clean getaway!

Taking it further   Collect sentences and phrases from the beginnings and endings of stories you read together. They can be drawn on to help write other stories.

Features of non-fiction

Non-fiction looks quite different from fiction, and you read it in a different way.

With **fiction**, you start at the beginning and read to the end.

With **non-fiction**, you can dip into the part you want to read. Non-fiction has 'signposts' to tell you where the information is. You don't have to start reading at the beginning.

Fiction or non-fiction?

- Which do you prefer to read?

  Non-fiction ☐   Fiction ☑

- Why?

  becus they are funxr
  then Non fiction is notasfunyo

Labels

- Look at this page from a non-fiction book. Fill in the labels with the words from this list:

chapter heading

subheading

caption

diagram

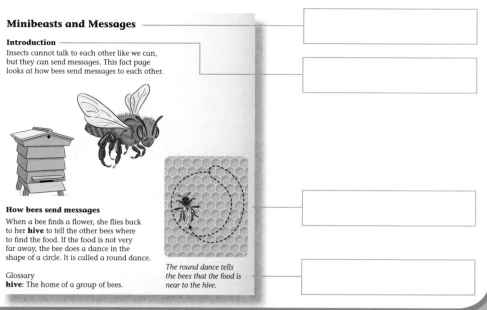

Minibeasts and Messages

Introduction
Insects cannot talk to each other like we can, but they can send messages. This fact page looks at how bees send messages to each other.

How bees send messages
When a bee finds a flower, she flies back to her **hive** to tell the other bees where to find the food. If the food is not very far away, the bee does a dance in the shape of a circle. It is called a round dance.

Glossary
hive: The home of a group of bees.

The round dance tells the bees that the food is near to the hive.

Supporting your child Help your child to find his/her way around non-fiction content (books and online) so that he/she can work independently to look for information.

Factual features

- The words below are all features you might find in non-fiction. What is each one for?

Heading _____

Subheading _____

Glossary _____

Index _____

Jolly joke

Why do you always walk with the right foot first?

When you put one foot forward the other is always left behind!

Writing non-fiction

- Write a few sentences to explain how something works; for example, the life cycle of a plant. Start with a heading and draw a diagram with a caption or labels.

_____

_____

_____

_____

_____

_____

_____

Taking it further   Set your child the challenge of finding specific information from a non-fiction book you have chosen. Encourage him/her to use the contents page, to scan and look out for headings, and to use the index to find key words and phrases.

Reading poetry

- Read this poem aloud several times and listen to the rhythm and the rhymes. Remember to use expression.

The lights from the parlour and kitchen shone out
Through the blinds and the windows and bars –
And high overhead, and all moving about,
There were thousands of millions of stars.

There ne'er were such thousands of leaves on a tree,
Nor of people in church or the park,
As the crowds of the stars looked down upon me,
And that glittered and winked in the dark.

The Dog, and the Plough, and the Hunter and all,
And the star of the sailor, and Mars –
These shone in the sky, and the pail by the wall
Would be half full of water and stars.

They saw me at last, and they chased me with cries,
And they soon had me packed into bed –
But the glory kept shining and bright in my eyes
And the stars going round in my head.

Robert Louis Stevenson (1809–1892)

What is it about?

- What title would you give the poem? _____

- Who is telling the story? _____

- Why did he want to tell us about his experience? _____

_____

Supporting your child   Poetry is another form of literature that is as important to read as fiction and non-fiction. It can also be a great source of pleasure, to read and to write. Play some word rhyming games with your child to encourage his/her interest in poetry.

The rhymes

- In the poem, which words rhyme at the end of the lines?

  Verse 1 _____ , _____ _____ , _____

  Verse 2 _____ , _____ _____ , _____

  Verse 3 _____ , _____ _____ , _____

  Verse 4 _____ , _____ _____ , _____

The rhythm

- Look at verses 1–3. How many syllables are there in lines 1 and 3?

- How many syllables are there in lines 2 and 4 of each verse?

Taking it further   Look out for collections of poetry for children in your local library or bookshops. Read some poems together and help your child find the kind of poetry he/she enjoys: classic or modern poetry, or a particular poet.

Answers

Page 4

Un– and dis–

unwell, unlucky, untidy, ungrateful
disobey, disagree, disappoint,
disappear

Choosing un– and dis– words

I felt really unwell so I went to visit
my doctor.
I am sorry to disappoint you but we
have no pencils left in the shop!
My sister's room looked very untidy,
so I tidied it for her.

Page 5

Re– means 'again' or 'back'

redo, refresh, return, reappear,
redecorate; check your child's writing.

Super– means 'big'

supermarket, superman,
supernatural, superstar; check your
child's writing.
a famous and well-known singer:
superstar
something that is beyond nature:
supernatural
a shop that is bigger than most:
supermarket
a man with more-than-ordinary
powers: superman

Page 6

–tion or –sion?

injection, extension, action,
comprehension, tension

Page 7

Fill the gaps

explosion, hesitate, infuse,
completion,
hesitation, complete

Write your own

Check that your child's sentences use
the –tion and –sion suffixes properly.

Page 8

Write the endings

picture, nature, future, mixture,
furniture, adventure

Page 9

Syllables

crea-ture, cul-ture, fix-ture,
frac-ture, mois-ture

Write your own

Check that your child's sentences use
the –ture ending properly.

Page 10

Apostrophes for contraction

I am – I'm; might have – might've;
I shall/will – I'll; they are – they're;
it is – it's; you are – you're;
does not – doesn't;
would have – would've;
will not – won't; did not – didn't;
could not – couldn't; we are – we're;
she is – she's; who is – who's

Page 11

Never write of!

ha, ha, ha, ha

Apostrophes for possession

the man's dinner, the tractor's wheel,
the child's doll, the teacher's pen,
the camel's hump

Page 12

Where are the articles?

An apple a day is good for you.
The school play started on time.
The supermarket will open at 8am.
An egg can be boiled before eating it.

Fill the gaps

a pen, a pan, a pot, an elephant,
a bird, an arrow
a beautiful girl, an open book,
a fiery dragon, an amazing school,
a delicious cake, an exciting play
The girl found a gold ring in an old
treasure box.

Page 13

Where are the prepositions?

The baby girl was born at 12 noon
on Monday.
They had a big party in August.
She'll serve you in ten minutes.
Her wedding was at 10am but she
was an hour late.

Changing times

We ate our breakfast before going
to the zoo.
I clean my teeth after I have eaten
my supper.
I have been waiting here since 9am!

Page 14

Where are the conjunctions?

The ginger cat hurriedly chased after
the tiny mouse but he was too fast!
He speedily ran across the room so
the cat could not find him. Later on,
the mouse laughed at the cat and
hid under the huge staircase.

Join the parts together

Our school netball team tries really
hard but we hardly ever win.
I would like to come but my mum
won't let me!
We wanted to win the football match
so we had to work as a team.
I will take off my boots so I don't make
a mess!
I want to have pizza for dinner and
ice cream for dessert.

Page 15

Where are the subordinate clauses?

Although it was night-time, the
street was full of people.
The dog barked when he saw his
owner.
Before dawn, the silver spaceship
landed somewhere in the woods.
While they were sleeping,
a rainbow arched across the sky.

Join the sentences together

The footballer scored although the
other team were playing well.
The monkey looked bored because
he wanted to live in the wild.
I had to share my cake because my
brother didn't have one.

Page 16

Highlight what people say

The teacher asked, "Which is farther
away – China or the sun?"
"China," answered Milly.
"Why do you think that?" asked the
teacher in surprise.
"Well, you can see the sun, but you
can't see China," Milly replied.
–, question mark, comma
You start a new line when another
person begins to speak.